Eye See You

A POSTER BOOK

What Are You Looking At?

Think of all of the things you do with your eyes: sensing light and dark, telling what color something is, and seeing where you are going. Eyes are amazing. Even though you have five senses, you depend on your sense of eyesight more than the other four.

For many animals living in the wild, eyesight is very important for hunting, finding food, and protecting themselves from other animals. But not all animals see the same way we do. To start with, they don't all have just two eyes. Many spiders have eight. But that doesn't mean they can see better than you can. A tarantula's eight eyes sense light and darkness but don't see much more than that.

Many animals can't see the same color range that you can, and dogs don't see colors at all! Bees and butterflies see lots of colors, but not the same ones that you see. For many animals, seeing in the dark is much more important than being able to see color. Tarsiers and owls have large, round eyes that collect lots of light from what's around them, helping them see things at night. Lions, leopards, cougars, and cheetahs are night creatures, too. The eyes of these big cats have a special structure that collects light and then reflects it, making it easier to see and hunt in the dark.

Some animals' eyes help protect them from enemies. A giraffe has one eye on each side of its head, allowing it to spot distant animals approaching from both the left and the right while it grazes on the grassy plains of Africa where it lives. The dark circles around a giant panda's eyes make it look more ferocious than it actually is, scaring off other animals.

You will find pictures of many amazing animals in this fun poster collection. And on the back of each poster, you can read more about the way each animal sees and uses its eyes. So go ahead, take a good look, and stare right back at these animal eyes!

Here's looking at you!

Tarsier

This little creature is a close relative of monkeys, gorillas, and chimpanzees. It is **arboreal** (spends its whole life in the trees) and lives in the tropical rain forests of Southeast Asia. Compared to its body size, no animal in the world has larger eyes than a tarsier.

Seeing in the Dark

The tarsier is **nocturnal** (sleeps during the day, active at night). During the day, it sleeps soundly in a thick clump of plants. When the sun goes down, this **predator** (hunter) wakes up and begins hunting for insects, lizards, and small birds. Because a tarsier's big, sharp eyes can take in a lot of light, they help the little hunter spot **prey** (animals being hunted) on even the darkest nights.

Animal in Action

It's close to midnight and the forest is pitch black. A hungry tarsier uses its good nighttime vision to spot a small beetle on a nearby tree trunk. It springs backward, twists around in midair, and lands feet first just a few inches from the insect. Before the beetle can escape, the tarsier grabs it and stuffs the prey into its mouth. Using its long tail and the sticky pads on its toes, the little hunter clings to the tree as it chews and swallows its dinner. Yum! Delicious!

Did You Know?

A tarsier can't move its eyes back and forth or up and down. Its eyes are too big. Luckily, a tarsier can **swivel** (turn in a circle) its head almost all the way around. This makes it easy for the little animal to spot prey.

photo © Frans Lanting • *Eye See You: A Poster Book*, Storey Publishing

Northern Saw-Whet Owl

This bird looks like a baby owl, but it may actually be fully grown. Northern saw-whet owls are tiny birds with very large eyes. They live in wooded areas throughout North America, but because they sleep the day away in tree holes, people almost never see them.

Those Amazing Eyes

Most birds' eyes are on the sides of their head, but an owl's eyes are on the front of its face. This helps an owl pinpoint the exact location of small animals as it flies overhead.

Because an owl's eyes are so large compared to its body size, the little bird can't move its eyeballs back and forth in its sockets. To look around, an owl must turn its head. Owls are famous for their ability to rotate their heads almost all the way around.

Animal in Action

It's a dark, moonless night, but a northern saw-whet owl has no trouble spotting a deer mouse creeping along the forest floor. The owl focuses on its prey, dives down, and grabs the unsuspecting mouse in its sharp claws. The mouse is small, but it's just the right size for the little owl and her nest of hungry **owlets** (baby owls).

What's in a Name?

The saw-whet owl gets its name from its early spring mating call. Some people say the owl's *skreigh-aw, skreigh-aw, skreigh-aw* call sounds like a saw being **whetted** (sharpened).

Hippopotamus

It's easy to see why a hippopotamus's eyes are so unusual. Like its nose (the two yellowish holes in front of the eyes) and ears, a hippo's eyes are located high on its head. This allows the gigantic African animal to keep most of its body underwater where it's protected from the sizzling sun.

Long, Lazy Days

A hippopotamus spends most of its day lounging in a shallow water hole. While it snoozes, a hippo's body automatically rises to the surface and breathes in every few minutes. The hippo doesn't even have to think about it.

Sometimes hippos come out of the water for a while. They lie close to shore and **wallow** (relax) in the mud. When a hippo really heats up, pink oil oozes out of its skin and acts like sunscreen!

Action-Packed Nights

At dusk, a hippo comes onto land and follows a well-worn path to its grazing grounds. The trail is marked with smelly **dung** (manure), so the hippo can find its way despite its poor eyesight. For most of the night, the hippo munches noisily on grass and leaves. Sometimes it lies down and takes a short nap. Just before sunrise, the hippo traces its trail back to the water and plunges in.

What's in a Name?

A hippopotamus looks like a huge horse and spends most of its time in African rivers or water holes. That's probably why its name is a combination of two Greek words that mean "river horse."

photo © Frans Lanting • Eye See You: A Poster Book, Storey Publishing

Black Panther

Most leopards have golden coats covered with dozens of dark spots, but every once in a while a leopard is born with solid black fur. Because many leopards live in dark forests and all leopards prefer to hunt at night, the black coloring can really come in handy.

A Closer Look at Leopards

Long ago, people didn't realize that leopards could be two different colors. They thought black leopards were a different type of animal, so they called them black panthers. When scientists discovered that black panthers are really leopards, they took a closer look at leopards all over the world. They realized that desert-dwelling leopards are usually pale yellow, while leopards living on grasslands are a deeper golden color.

Invisible Eyes

During the day, the pupils in a leopard's eyes become thin slits so they don't let in too much light. But at night, when the light is low, the pupils open wide and let the light flow in. This change makes it possible for leopards to see in near-lightless conditions. It also makes their eyes very dark, so that they become nearly invisible to **prey** (animals being hunted). If scientists shine a spotlight on a leopard's eyes, they glow so brightly that they can be seen through very dense forests.

Did You Know?

The tongues of all cats are covered with tough, backward-slanted bumps. Cats use them to lick even the tiniest bits of flesh off the bones of their prey.

photo © Tom Brakefield/CORBIS • *Eye See You: A Poster Book*, Storey Publishing

Tarantula

Like most spiders, tarantulas have eight, closely clustered eyes — two large ones and six small ones. (Two of the smaller eyes are not visible in this photo.) With so many eyes, you might think tarantulas have excellent eyesight, but think again. These large spiders must rely on their sense of touch to catch **prey** (animals being hunted).

Animal in Action

In the late afternoon, a tarantula emerges from its underground **burrow** (hole in the ground) and begins to hunt for grasshoppers, beetles, **sow bugs** (small insects similar to lice), and other small creatures. As soon as it detects the tiny vibrations an insect makes as it scurries along the ground, the tarantula prepares to attack. When the prey is within its grasp, the spider lunges forward, grabs the prey, and sinks its fangs into the victim. As **venom** (poison) flows though the tarantula's fangs and into the insect's body, the prey is paralyzed. Then the tarantula eats the insect.

Home Sweet Home

Tarantulas are hairy spiders that live in warm, dry **environments** (an animal's natural surroundings) all over the world. In North America, they can be found in the south and southwestern United States and throughout Mexico.

Did You Know?

Although tarantulas are ferocious **predators** (hunters), they are harmless to humans. Their bite is no more painful than a bee sting. Some people even keep tarantulas as pets.

photo © agefotostock/SuperStock • *Eye See You: A Poster Book*, Storey Publishing

Polar Bear and Cub

Polar bears are the largest land **carnivores** (meat eaters) in the world and spend their whole lives patrolling the ice **floes** (large sheets of floating ice) and frozen shores of the Arctic. Female polar bears make good mothers. They stay with their cubs for two or more years, keeping them safe and teaching them how to hunt.

Those Amazing Eyes

Polar bears are excellent hunters and have good vision. They have special **membranes** (thin, clear layers of tissue) over their eyes to protect them from the sun's glare and dangerous ultraviolet (UV) rays. It's a bit like having built-in sunglasses. Because their eyes face forward, they are good at judging distances.

The Perfect Body

A polar bear's fluffy, white coat keeps out the cold and helps the bear blend in with its surroundings. Underneath the fur, the bear's skin is black, helping it soak up the sun's warm rays. This, and a thick layer of fat under the skin, help it survive average winter temperatures of −30°F (−35°C).

A polar bear sees and hears about as well as a person, but it has a stronger sense of smell. A polar bear can sniff out a seal — its favorite food — more than 20 miles away!

Did You Know?

Polar bears are patient hunters. They may wait near a seal's breathing hole for hours. When a seal finally comes up for air, the polar bear kills it instantly and eats its thick, rich fat. A polar bear may eat as much as 150 pounds of meat in one sitting.

photo © Steve Bloom • *Eye See You A: Poster Book*, Storey Publishing

Cougar

What is this large cat with the striking green eyes? It depends on whom you ask. Puma, mountain lion, panther, catamount — people use many different names to describe the animal scientists call the cougar.

Staring Down Its Prey

Like its cat relatives, a cougar can see in the dark and depends on its keen eyesight and good hearing to find **prey** (animals being hunted). It scans the horizon for prey, and then stares at the intended victim until it is ready to attack. Its favorite food is white-tailed deer, but it also hunts opossums, rabbits, beavers, raccoons, and mice. If food is in short supply, it will dine on birds and insects.

Once in a while, a cougar is able to kill a moose or elk. After the cougar eats its fill, it buries the rest of the **carcass** (dead body) to hide it from other animals. A few days later, the cougar will dig up the body and finish it off.

Home Sweet Home

There isn't much chance you'll ever run into a lion or a leopard, a jaguar or a tiger. Those big cats live in far-off places. But the cougar lives right here in North America. Cougars were once in danger of disappearing from Earth forever, but today small numbers of them live in forests and swamps as well as on grasslands and mountain slopes across the continent.

Did You Know?

You won't find cougars by listening for a roar. Unlike lions and leopards, cougars purr like pets.

photo © Frans Lanting • *Eye See You: A Poster Book*, Storey Publishing

Red-Fronted Brown Lemur

Like most of its monkey relatives, lemurs live in trees. Red-fronted brown lemurs like this one live in the forests of Madagascar, a large island off the east coast of Africa.

A Day in the Life

Red-fronted brown lemurs usually live in small groups. They awake at the crack of dawn and start searching for leaves, seedpods, stems, flowers, bark, fruit, insects, and birds' eggs. As lemurs move through the treetops, they grip branches with their hands and feet, and they use their long tails to stay balanced. Because a lemur's eyes are on the front of its head, not the sides, it can judge distances well, making it easy to leap from tree to tree.

Grooming Buddies

Like monkeys, red-fronted brown lemurs spend time **grooming** (cleaning) one another while they rest. Monkeys use their fingers to pick insects, dirt, and bits of dead skin out of their friends' fur, but lemurs use their teeth. They have six lower teeth that stick straight out from their jaw and work just like a comb. Grooming is more than just a way to stay clean. It is a way of expressing friendship and establishing trust.

Did You Know?

The red-fronted brown lemur is about the size of a house cat. And, like the house cat, its eyes shine bright yellow in the light.

photo © Jon Atkinson • *Eye See You: A Poster Book*, Storey Publishing

Giraffe

All you see behind this giraffe is clear blue sky. That's because giraffes are the tallest animals in the world. They tower high above the plains of their African home. Using their long tongues, giraffes can easily grab leaves and twigs that other animals can't reach.

Exceptional Eyes

Giraffes have excellent eyesight, and when paired with their height, they have a real advantage over other animals. A giraffe can recognize its mate from half a mile away, and it can see some colors. Because a giraffe's eyes are located on the sides of its head, it can easily see far to the right and left.

On the Spot

Every giraffe has its own **unique** (one-of-a-kind) pattern of spots. When scientists study giraffes, they use the patterns to tell the animals apart.

A giraffe's spots help it blend in with its surroundings. It might seem impossible to hide an animal as large as a giraffe, but people often report mistaking a giraffe for an old, dead tree. They don't realize what they're looking at until the "tree" suddenly starts walking away!

What's in a Name?

It's a giraffe's speed, not its height, that gives the animal its name. "Giraffe" comes from an Arab word that means "the one that walks very fast."

White's Tree Frog

Like most frogs, the White's tree frog hears well and has a good sense of touch. But the shy, plump creature's most important sense is its eyesight. It relies on its big, bulging eyes to catch flying and crawling insects.

Plump Little Guy

The White's tree frog lives in the tropical rain forests of Australia and Indonesia where it finds plenty of insects like locusts, moths, and roaches to eat. The little **amphibian** (a cold-blooded animal that spends at least part of its life in the water) has a large appetite and is a very good eater. It is known to eat nonstop and can grow as large as a baseball. Its fatty folds of skin have earned it the nick-name "dumpy tree frog."

The Skin They're In

Like some lizards, White's tree frogs can change the color of their skin. Most of the time, they are bluish green. But depending on their mood and their surroundings, they can turn their smooth, waxy skin many different shades of green and blue. They can also become red-dish or purplish in color. And when they're upset or sick, they turn dark brown.

Did You Know?

Even though White's tree frogs can hop, they also move in other ways. When White's tree frogs aren't in a hurry, they may walk slowly hand-over-hand. When they need to climb slippery tree trunks, they use the suction cups on their large toes.

photo © Stephen Cooper/Getty Images • *Eye See You: A Poster Book,* Storey Publishing

Lion

When people use the expression "king of the jungle," they are usually talking about lions. These large cats don't live in jungles or rain forests, however. They live on the **plains** (flat or rolling treeless areas) of Africa.

Eyes Fit for a King

Lions have larger eyes than other animals of their size, and their eyesight is five times better than a person's. Lions' eyes do not glow in the dark, but their eyes do have a special coating that reflects moonlight and helps them see in the dark. This is especially helpful when hunting at night.

A Lion's Life

Most cats live alone, but lions live in groups called **prides.** A pride may have as many as forty members, but more than half are cubs or youngsters. Lions usually spend more than twenty hours a day resting or sleeping, so they must use their hunting time wisely.

Lions hunt in groups and often attack zebras, giraffes, hippopotamuses, and other large **prey** (animals being hunted). Lions carefully **stalk** (follow) and surround their prey, lunging forward at the last moment. While several lions pin down the prey, one kills the animal by biting its neck or covering its mouth so it can't breathe.

Did You Know?

Of the four cats that can roar — the lion, the tiger, the leopard, and the jaguar — the lion roars the most. Its roar is strong enough to raise a cloud of dust and can be heard five miles away.

White-Tailed Eagle

Don't mess with me! That's the message we seem to get from this white-tailed eagle's stare. The sharp eyes are also extremely good at spotting fish from a distance. Found mostly along northern Europe's rocky coastlines in the summer, the large bird migrates to inland lakes and wetlands in the winter.

The Eyes Have It

An eagle's eyes contain many more sensory cells than a person's eyes, so the birds can see distant objects much more clearly. Scientists think an eagle's vision is about six times better than a person's.

Think of a chickadee or a robin. Its eyes are located on the sides of its head. But an eagle's eyes are far enough forward that it can see in three dimensions. This helps an eagle judge distances so it can catch **prey** (animals being hunted) more easily.

Extra Eyelids

An eagle's eyes have two kinds of eyelids. The outer eyelids are similar to yours, but they close from the bottom. An eagle shuts these eyelids when it wants to go to sleep. An eagle's inner eyelids are **transparent,** which means the bird can see through them. They close sideways and blink every few seconds to keep an eagle's eyes moist and clean.

Did You Know?

A hungry young eaglet could accidentally jab a parent in the eye as it lunges for food. To protect themselves, adult eagles often close their transparent inner eyelids while they feed their young.

photo © agefotostock/SuperStock • *Eye See You: A Poster Book,* Storey Publishing

Giant Panda

Giant pandas live in China's cool, misty, mountain forests and spend most of their time munching on bamboo. At one time, thousands of pandas lived on Earth, but today they are **endangered** (struggling to survive).

Eyes That Send a Message

Giant pandas have an excellent sense of smell, but they don't see very well. Still, it is their amazing eyes that may save them. The large, dark rings around a giant panda's eyes make the gentle plant eater look ferocious to large **predators** (hunters). Yet, those same circles make a panda look cuddly to us. Predators don't attack pandas, and we fight to save them because of what we see in their eyes.

Animal in Action

A giant panda wakes from its afternoon nap and begins to search for food. Now and then, it pauses to dine on a plant bulb or a bird's egg, but what it really wants is bamboo. When it finds some, the panda sits down and grabs a few stems at a time. It stuffs the plants into its mouth and crushes them with its powerful jaws. To get the 20 to 40 pounds of food it needs each day, a giant panda must **forage** (look for food) for 10 to 16 hours.

Did You Know?

The giant panda is a member of the bear family, but its eyes aren't like those of other bears. A panda's eyes are shaped like a cat's, so it's no surprise that the Chinese name for these big forest creatures means "giant cat bear."

Borean Orangutan

Like gorillas and chimpanzees, orangutans are great apes. Great apes are our closest living relatives. Because their facial expressions and body language are so similar to ours, it sometimes seems like we can tell exactly how they feel. This orangutan seems to be saying, "Give me a break!"

Keep Your Eye on the Branch

An orangutan spends most of its time searching the rain forest for fruit, leaves, ferns, insects, and birds' eggs. This **herbivore** (plant eater) depends on its forward-facing eyes to judge distances accurately. Without its amazing eyes, an orangutan would have trouble traveling from tree to tree. One wrong move and the big red ape could end up crashing to the forest floor.

Two Kinds of Orangutans

At one time, orangutans lived in tropical rain forests throughout Southeast Asia. But today they survive on just two small islands in that region — Sumatra and Borneo. Sumatran orangutans have mostly orange hair, and the males have oval faces. Bornean orangutans, like the one shown in this photo, have mostly brown hair. Adult males have round faces.

Did You Know?

At night an orangutan sleeps on a platform of twigs it built in the fork of a tree. When the weather is cold or rainy, an orangutan stays warm and cozy by covering itself with a blanket of leaves.

African Elephant

Elephants are the largest animals on land. African elephants, like this one, live on the **savannas** (grasslands with scattered trees) of East Africa. They are more than 11 feet tall and weigh as much as 12,000 pounds! The elephant's ear is as big as a blanket. An elephant's giant tusks weigh about as much as you do!

Keeping Eyes Safe

Elephants have excellent senses of smell and hearing, but their vision isn't nearly as good. Still, an elephant's eyes are well protected. Long, thick lashes keep dust and dirt out. When an elephant is feeding in dense, low bushes, a layer of tough skin closes tightly over each delicate eyeball.

Happy or Sad, Calm or Mad

It's easy to tell how an elephant feels. When an elephant feels calm or safe, it holds its ears flat against its body. When an elephant is angry or frightened, it holds its ears out straight. When two elephants are happy to see each other, they flap their ears, click their tusks, and make rumbling noises. They may also wrap their trunks together or touch one another on the forehead with their trunk.

Did You Know?

Elephants' big ears pick up sounds that most animals can't hear. When an elephant wants to cool off, it flaps its ears so excess heat can escape from its body.

photo © Tim Flach/Getty Images • *Eye See You: A Poster Book*, Storey Publishing

Grass Snake

This snake's eyes really are staring at you! A grass snake never closes its eyes, not even when it's asleep. That's because it doesn't have eyelids. Instead, each eye is protected by a tough, clear scale. When the snake **molts** (sheds its skin), its old eye scales pop off right along with the rest of its outer covering.

Home Sweet Home

Grass snakes live in central and southern Europe, northern Africa, and central Asia. They are excellent swimmers and can stay underwater for up to an hour. Their favorite foods include frogs, fish, and salamanders, but they also eat mice and small birds.

A Talented Tongue

With a lightning-quick flick of the tongue, this grass snake can know everything it needs to about its surroundings. Like most other snakes, a grass snake's extraordinary tongue can taste and smell at the same time.

Did You Know?

When a grass snake feels threatened, it puffs up its body and hisses loudly. If the attacker isn't scared, the snake releases a terrible-smelling liquid. And if that doesn't send the enemy running, the grass snake rolls over and plays dead. It remains silent and still with its mouth open and its tongue hanging out until the **predator** (hunter) loses interest and goes away.

Alpaca

Most of time, alpacas are kind and calm — as long as you know how to treat them. As you can see in this picture, an alpaca's large, dark eyes look very friendly. Don't stare at this animal too long, though. Eye contact is a major threat to an alpaca. It may kick at you or even spit in your face!

Those Amazing Eyes

An alpaca's sharp eyes and long neck help it spot **pumas** (large cats that are also called cougars), leopards, and other hungry **predators** (hunters) lurking among the boulders that cover the rocky slopes of its mountain home. Because an alpaca's eyes are set far apart, it can see far to the right and left as it grazes on grasses, weeds, shrubs, and trees.

Home Sweet Home

Alpacas come from the Andes Mountains of South America. Their thick, woolly coats are perfect for the long, cold winters, and their **hoofed feet** (feet made of the same hard material as your fingernails, like goat's and sheep's feet) have no trouble on the slippery, snowy mountain slopes.

Did You Know?

Alpacas are members of the camel family. Their closest relatives are llamas. Alpacas are smaller than llamas, and they have longer, softer wool. Because the alpacas' fur makes such good sweaters, people have been keeping them as farm animals for more than 5,000 years!

Domestic Cat

Ever seen a cat this close up? It's just the kitty next door, but it does look a little threatening. A **domestic** (lives with or serves humans) cat's forward-facing eyes, sharp claws, rotating ears, and hunter's **stance** (way of standing) remind us that the members of the cat family are among the world's fiercest hunters.

Glow-in-the-Dark Eyes

If you have a pet cat, try this experiment. On a dark night, shine a bright light at your cat's eyes. You'll see that they glow in the dark. What causes this? A mirror-like **membrane** (a thin, clear layer of tissue) inside a cat's eye collects light from the cat's surroundings and then reflects it. The magnified light helps a cat see well in the dark. All cats, including the bigger ones like lions and leopards, have this membrane.

Cats Through History

According to scientists, people have been living with cats for at least 8,000 years. At first, they probably kept them in their homes just to catch mice, rats, and other pests, but by 4,000 years ago, cats had become true pets.

In ancient Egypt, some people worshipped cats. When a pet cat died, its body was carefully prepared for burial and the whole family went into **mourning** (a time of sadness after a death). Scientists have found thousands of cat mummies.

Did You Know?

Cats don't walk the same way you do. They walk on their toes with the back parts of their feet raised.

photo © SuperStock • *Eye See You: A Poster Book,* Storey Publishing

Gorilla

Thanks to movies and comic books, gorillas have gotten a bad reputation. They really aren't as mean and ferocious as you might think. Most of the time, these shy, intelligent creatures live quiet, peaceful lives in the forests of central Africa.

A Gorilla's Eyes

Compared to the size of a gorilla's head, a gorilla's eyes are fairly small. That doesn't mean gorillas have poor eyesight, however. Because their eyes are set close together, they can judge distances well. They can also see a full range of colors.

A Day in the Life

Gorillas rise early and spend the morning wandering the forest looking for tasty leaves, stems, and fruits. Their favorite foods include bamboo, wild celery, and blackberries. Thanks to the position of their eyes, they can easily reach across a branch to grab for leaves without losing their balance.

In the middle of the day, the gentle beasts rest and play in the warm sun. If it's raining, they sit under trees, with their knees pulled close to their chests, and wait for the storm to end. In the late afternoon, gorillas gather more food. As the sun goes down, they stop wherever they are and build nests out of twigs and leaves. Then they lie down and sleep soundly until a new day dawns.

Did You Know?

An adult male gorilla is called a **silverback** because he has silver-colored fur on his back. Each gorilla **troop**, or group, has a silverback as its leader.

photo © JH Pete Carmichael/Getty Images • *Eye See You: A Poster Book*, Storey Publishing

Gray Wolf

Thanks to nursery rhymes and folktales, most people think of wolves as mean and sneaky, and so these peering eyes may look a little scary. Wolves are really no different from other large **predators** (hunters), though. They need to hunt and kill **prey** (animals being hunted) to stay alive.

Eight Eyes Are Better Than Two

Gray wolves have a keen sense of smell, and excellent hearing and eyesight. Their superior senses are very good at finding prey. Wolves usually hunt in packs. By working together, they can attack **elk** (similar to large deer), deer, moose, and **bison** (similar to buffalo). When wolves hunt alone, they focus on birds, fish, snakes, and other small animals.

Animal in Action

As a pack of wolves jogs across a snow-covered plain, the leader suddenly stops, raises its nose, and sniffs the air. The other wolves sniff, too. They smell a herd of elk just over the next hill.

The wolves spread out in all directions. When the elk are in the hunters' sights, the attack begins. The wolves startle the elk, and the herd scatters. The wolves spot the weakest animal and chase it. The leader jumps on the elk's back, knocks it down, and kills it.

Did You Know?

At one time, gray wolves were common throughout North America, Europe, and Asia. Then people killed them by the thousands, and by the 1900s, gray wolves were in danger of disappearing from Earth forever. Finally, people fought to save wolves, and today the howling hunters are making a comeback.

photo © Monty Sloan • *Eye See You: A Poster Book*, Storey Publishing

Gray Crowned Crane

You're not likely to see this startling creature with the misty gray eyes in your backyard! The gray crowned crane lives in the wetlands and grassy flatlands of the African countries of Uganda, Congo, Kenya, and Tanzania.

Those Amazing Eyes

Most birds have excellent eyesight, and gray crowned cranes are no exception. Their eyes might seem small, but they are super sharp and can see a full range of colors. These birds have no trouble seeing what's in front of them, and they can see far to the right and left without moving their head.

Animal in Action

The sky suddenly darkens as a huge, beautiful bird flies overhead, blocking out the sun. The gray crowned crane flaps its huge wings and then glides gracefully as it searches for a place to land. The bird's long neck stretches forward, and its long, sticklike legs drag behind.

When the crane's sharp eyes spot a grassy marsh, it slowly descends, landing with only a slight splash. As the bird wades silently through the shallow water, it occasionally stops and stomps its large, slender feet. If it turns up an insect, frog, or fish, the crane quickly snatches the **prey** (animal being hunted) and swallows it whole.

Did You Know?

Gray crowned cranes really know how to get down and boogie. Their elaborate dances include head bobbing, wing fluttering, leaps, and bows. Native Africans borrowed some of the crane's moves and used them in their own tribal dances.

Three-Horned Chameleon

The three-horned chameleon is named for the trio of inch-long structures sticking out of its head, but its eyes are its most interesting feature. The three-horned chameleon comes from the rain forests of East Africa, but people all over the world keep these medium-sized lizards as pets.

Those Amazing Eyes

A chameleon's eyeballs are mounted on short stalks that stick out of its head. Its eyes can rotate in almost any direction and move independently, so the chameleon can look in two different directions at the same time. This special ability makes it easy for the **reptile** (a cold-blooded animal that lives on land and has scaly skin) to quickly scan its surroundings.

Animal in Action

Hour after hour, a hungry three-horned chameleon quietly perches on a high branch. Its head stays perfectly still, but its eyes slowly **swivel** (turn in a circle). One eye looks up, while the other looks down. One eye stares straight ahead, while the other glances over the chameleon's shoulder. The instant an insect flies by, the lizard's long, sticky tongue darts out of its mouth and catches the **prey** (animal being hunted). The chameleon swallows the insect whole.

Did You Know?

Most of the time, a three-horned chameleon is green, but when it feels angry or frightened it may turn brown or black.

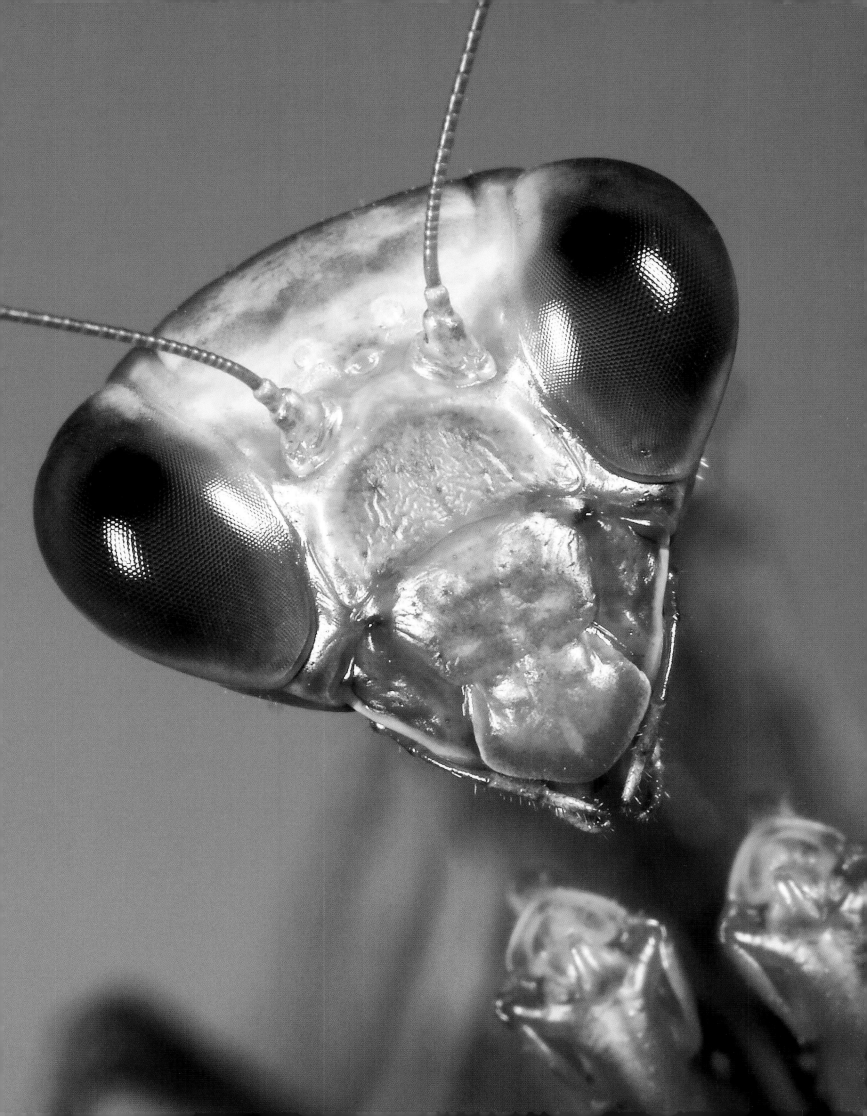

Praying Mantis

This praying mantis's eyes might look solid, but they are actually **compound eyes** that are made up of many tiny units. Each unit sees just one small piece of the insect's surroundings. Most insects have compound eyes.

Mantis Mania

Praying mantises live all over the world, and they eat almost anything they can catch. Most of the time, praying mantises eat other insects, but they may also gobble up small snakes, lizards, tree frogs, and small birds. Gardeners like praying mantises because they eat many of the insects that destroy plants growing in our gardens.

Extraordinary Eyes

A praying mantis has excellent vision. Its eyes can spot the slightest movements up to 60 feet away. And because a praying mantis can rotate its head much farther than any other insect, it can see in almost any direction without moving its body. As a praying mantis slowly **swivels** (turns in a circle) its triangular-shaped head, it can judge the distance between itself and any object.

What's in a Name?

The praying mantis's name comes from the way it holds its body as it waits for **prey** (animals being hunted) to pass by. Hour after hour, a praying mantis remains silent and still with its short front legs raised and folded. The insect may look as if it's praying, but it's really trying to blend in with its surroundings.

photo © agefotostock/SuperStock • *Eye See You: A Poster Book*, Storey Publishing

Japanese Macaques

Japanese macaques are often called snow monkeys, and with good reason. No other monkeys live so far north and see as much snow. It's easy to admire these tough, little monkeys, but their harsh habitat isn't the only reason people are so fond of them. Their hairless, red faces and expressive eyes remind us of what we see when we look in the mirror.

Home Sweet Home

Japanese macaques live in forested areas all over Japan, but it's the monkeys living on the snowy slopes of Honshu Island that get the most attention. For most of the year, their thick fur is enough to keep them warm. When winter temperatures dip below freezing, the monkeys make regular visits to the area's natural hot springs. There's nothing quite like a nice, warm bath.

Keeping an Eye Out for Food

Snow monkeys depend on their excellent vision to find food. In spring and summer, they search for young leaves, flowers, and shoots. In autumn, they eat mostly fruit. In winter, they focus their **foraging** (search for food) on buds and bark. They also eat crabs and bird eggs whenever they can.

Did You Know?

Some monkeys live alone or in small groups, but Japanese macaques live in very large groups. A typical **troop** (group) may have as many as thirty monkeys. Most of the members are adult females and their children. One adult male leads the troop. He usually gets help from two or three other males.

photo © Steve Bloom • *Eye See You: A Poster Book*, Storey Publishing

Leopard

The leopard is a master of disguise. When it crouches down in tall grass or lies quietly on a tree branch, its spotted coat makes it nearly invisible.

Home Sweet Home

Leopards live in southern Asia and central Africa. They are adaptable creatures that can survive in a variety of habitats. Leopards can be found in forests or on grasslands. Some even live in deserts or on rocky mountain slopes. A leopard's size and food choices vary from place to place.

Animal in Action

As the sun goes down on an African plain, a leopard wakes from its nap. From its seat on the lowest branch of a tree, the hunter scans the **savanna** (a grassland with scattered trees) with its sharp eyes. It quickly spots a young **impala** (a kind of antelope) that has strayed from its herd. Carefully and quietly, the leopard climbs to the ground and sneaks toward its target. The hunter lunges forward, knocks down the helpless impala, and quickly breaks its neck. The leopard spends the next few hours eating its kill.

What's in a Name?

Long ago, people thought the leopard was a cross between a lion and a panther. That's why the word "leopard" is a combination of the the Latin word for "lion" and an ancient word meaning "panther."

Red-Eyed Tree Frog

I t's easy to see how the red-eyed tree frog got its name. It has bulging red eyes and lives in trees. Scientists think the frog's bright, bold eyes startle predators just long enough for the little frog to make its escape.

Those Amazing Eyes

The red-eyed tree frog certainly isn't the only frog with bulging eyeballs. Most frogs have them. They allow the little **amphibians** (cold-blooded animals that spend at least part of their life in the water) to see far to the right and left, while staying perfectly still. Most frogs also have thin, partly transparent inner eyelids. When they are shut, these eyelids protect the frog's eyes without blocking its view of the world.

Home Sweet Home

The red-eyed tree frog lives in the lowland tropical rain forests of Central America and northern South America. During the day, the frog uses its suction-cup feet to attach itself to the underside of a leaf, where it can sleep in safety. At night, the red-eyed tree frog climbs and hops around the rain forest **canopy** (top layer of branches), catching insects with its long, sticky tongue. It also eats worms, spiders, and even smaller frogs.

Did You Know?

A red-eyed tree frog can change the color of its skin from green to reddish brown to match its mood or blend in with its surroundings.

photo © Tim Flach/Getty Images • *Eye See You: A Poster Book*, Storey Publishing

Green Iguana

This beautifully colored lizard lives in the tropical rain forests of Central America and South America. An immovable eyelid at the top and a movable eyelid at the bottom protect the green iguana's eyes, which are very important parts of its body.

At Home in the Forest

A green iguana spends most of its time in rainforest treetops. Its keen hearing and excellent eyesight help it spot enemies before they get too close. If a snake or weasel attacks, an iguana may dive to the forest floor. An iguana can fall up to 50 feet without getting hurt!

Animal in Action

It's mid-morning in the tropical rain forest. A green iguana drags its sluggish body to a sunny spot and basks in the sun's warm rays. It isn't long before the cold-blooded creature is ready for action. It climbs through the treetops in search of tasty leaves and fruits. Now and then, it nips at an insect or steals a bird's egg.

Suddenly, the iguana stops eating and scans its surroundings. It spots a harpy eagle flying in its direction. As the **predator** (hunter) closes in, the iguana whips its sharp tail back and forth. The eagle grabs the tail and flies away, but the iguana stays safe. Its tail can snap off and then grow back.

Did You Know?

Green iguanas like the water and are good swimmers. They can hold their breath for more than an hour and can even sleep underwater.

photo © Steve Bloom • *Eye See You: A Poster Book*, Storey Publishing

Labrador Retriever

ho could resist this cute, cuddly puppy? Like a human baby, the large, wide-set eyes of this little yellow Labrador retriever make it irresistible.

The Perfect Pet

Labrador retrievers are one of more than 300 **breeds** (kinds) of dogs that exist worldwide. Some dogs have been bred to guard property, while others do their best performing at a dog show. Labrador retrievers have just the right blend of traits to make them great pets. They are gentle and intelligent. They like to please their owners, and they have no trouble bonding with family members. Most Labrador retrievers are black, but yellow Labs and chocolate Labs are becoming more and more popular.

A Hunter's Eyes

Labrador retrievers have sharp eyes and a keen sense of smell. Even though dogs can't see colors, Labrador retrievers are better than people at detecting moving objects, especially at night or in dark places. This is why they were originally bred to help their masters hunt. After the owner had shot a bird or other small animal, the dog would find and **retrieve** (fetch) the dead or wounded game.

What's in a Name?

You might guess that Labrador retrievers were first bred in Labrador, Canada, but they weren't. They actually come from the nearby island of Newfoundland.

photo © Nick Ridley • *Eye See You: A Poster Book,* Storey Publishing

Baby Orangutan

Can you guess what this little orangutan is thinking? At first glance, it seems like it might be up to no good. Like people, orangutans are highly intelligent, so this little one really could be dreaming up some sort of wild plan.

Those Amazing Eyes

What is it that makes us wonder what this orangutan is thinking? It's the eyes. Like human babies, young orangutans have large, expressive eyes and long eyelashes. They are what make a little orangutan so adorable.

Growing Up Orangutan

An orangutan mother spends a lot of time caring for her youngsters. Starting when she is about 10 years old, a female orangutan has a baby every 5 or 6 years. Each newborn is helpless and clings to its mother's stomach 24 hours a day. Like all **mammals** (warm-blooded animals that have hair or fur and feed their young milk), it feeds on milk made in its mother's body. The youngster begins to eat solid food when it's about a year old, but it continues to drink some of its mother's milk for another 3 years.

When a young male is ready to survive on his own, he leaves his mother. A young female stays close by and watches her mother raise a new baby, so she can learn to care for the babies she will have one day.

What's in a Name?

The native peoples of Indonesia and Malaysia noticed that orangutans look a lot like people. They called the great apes "orang-hutan," which meant "people of the forest."

photo © Tim Flach/Getty Images • *Eye See You: A Poster Book,* Storey Publishing

Poison Dart Frog and Spactacled Caiman

You might wonder why this **caiman** (a close relative of alligators and crocodiles) doesn't whip its head around and make a quick meal of the little frog. The frog's bright colors send the **predator** (hunter) a warning message: "Don't eat me." A poison dart frog's skin is so poisonous that it could easily kill a caiman.

Day and Night

During the day, poison dart frogs are active, but caimans usually aren't. From its perch, the hungry frog in the photograph uses its keen eyesight to spot flying insects and other tasty treats. When the sun goes down, the poison dart frog hops onto a nearby plant and falls asleep. The caiman slips into the water and searches for **prey** (animals being hunted). Its sharp eyes work best at night, when the light is low.

Home Sweet Home

Poison dart frogs and spectacled caimans live in the tropical rain forests of Central America and South America. Poison dart frogs live throughout the forest, but caimans prefer to stay near rivers or wetlands.

What's in a Name?

The spectacled caiman gets its name from the bony ridge around its eyes. The ridge makes the reptile look like it's wearing a pair of **spectacles**, or eyeglasses.

The mission of Storey Publishing is to serve our customers
by publishing practical information that encourages
personal independence in harmony with the environment.

Edited by Deborah Balmuth and Sarah Guare
Art direction by Vicky Vaughn
Text design and production by Kristy MacWilliams
Cover photograph © Tim Flach/Getty Images
Additional interior photographs © Frans Lanting, title;
© Art Wolfe/Getty Images, intro page, top;
© Jon Atkinson, intro page, bottom; © Steve Bloom, above image.

Storey books are available for special premium and promotional uses and for customized editions.
For further information, please call 1-800-793-9396.

Printed in the Hong Kong by Elegance
10 9 8 7 6 5 4 3 2 1

Other Storey Titles You Will Enjoy

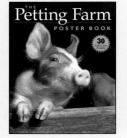

The Petting Farm Poster Book. Thirty pull-out posters feature beautifully reproduced full-color images of sweet chicks, ducklings, kids, lambs, calves, foals, piglets, rabbits, and more. The back of each poster contains fun facts about the animal's breed, habits, and history. 64 pages. Paperback. ISBN 1-58017-597-X.

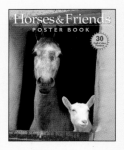

Horses & Friends Poster Book. These 30 full-color posters feature horses with ponies, dogs, cats, goats, and other adorable companion animals. The irresistible posters are made for pulling out and decorating bedrooms, playrooms, lockers, or stables. 64 pages. Paperback. ISBN 1-58017-580-5.

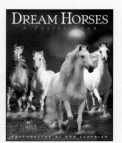

Dream Horses: A Poster Book. Celebrate the beauty, the power, and the majesty of horses with 30 full-color, large-format posters of horses in captivating, dreamlike scenes created by master photographer Bob Langrish. Inspiring text accompanies each fantastical poster. 64 pages. Paperback. ISBN 1-58017-547-0.

The Horse Breeds Poster Book. Suitable for hanging on bedroom walls, in school lockers, or even in barns, these 30 posters show horses in a range of colors and sizes, at work and in competition. Facts about the pictured horse breeds are included on the back of each poster. 64 pages. Paperback. ISBN 1-58017-507-4.

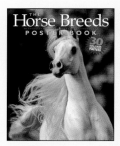

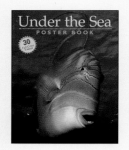

Under the Sea Poster Book. Bring the aquarium home with 30 full-color, pull-out portraits of fantastic sea creatures that kids love, plus all the fun facts that make each ocean resident unique and exciting. 64 pages. Paperback. ISBN 1-58017-623-2.

These and other books by Storey Publishing are available wherever quality books are sold or by calling 1-800-441-5700. Visit us at www.storey.com